JAZZ JUNIOR

10 STANDARDS FOR SOLO OR UNISON SINGING

	TITLE	ARRANGER	PAGE
1.	Bye Bye Blackbird	Jay Althouse	5
2.	Duke's Place	Russell Robinson	10
3.	Fascinating Rhythm	Michele Weir	17
4.	It Don't Mean a Thing (If It Ain't Got That Swing)	Michele Weir	23
5.	Jeepers Creepers	Jay Althouse	29
6.	Let's Call the Whole Thing Off	Russell Robinson	37
7.	Misty	Lisa DeSpain	44
8.	Orange Colored Sky	Kirby Shaw	48
9.	Over the Rainbow	Kirby Shaw	54
10.	Straighten Up and Fly Right	Lisa DeSpain	58

Reproducible Singer Pages (available online) may be duplicated, displayed, and posted for the use of one school/organization.

Alfred

alfred.com

© 2022 by Alfred Music
All Rights Reserved. Printed in USA.

Book & Online PDF/Audio (00-49866)	Book & Online PDF (00-49865)	Online Audio (00-49867)	Enhanced CD (00-49868)
ISBN-10: 1-4706-5157-2	ISBN-10: 1-4706-5156-4		1-4706-5199-8
ISBN-13: 978-1-4706-5157-2	ISBN-13: 978-1-4706-5156-5		978-1-4706-5199-2

All Cover Art Resources © Getty Images.

FOREWORD
by Michele Weir

Welcome to *Jazz Junior*! This collection offers a sampling of ten well-known standards from the Great American Songbook, with inventive arrangements from leading vocal jazz arrangers.

Jazz Junior is designed to educate and inspire vocal soloists and developing choirs in the idiom of vocal jazz. It offers the unique opportunity to study and perform stylistically authentic arrangements without the harmonic complexity often associated with vocal jazz literature. Each piece features creative use of single melodic lines which can be sung by either choral ensembles (in unison) or vocal soloists, helping to make jazz highly accessible.

REHEARSAL & PERFORMANCE IDEAS

Listening

Listening to music is always a good idea when learning a new musical style. Guided listening can be integrated into rehearsals on a regular basis, especially if excerpts are limited to short segments rather than long passages of music.

Guided Listening Activity: First, set the stage by establishing a standard for full attention on listening, and no talking. Then, play a 1–2 minute excerpt of any song from *Jazz Junior* as performed by a prominent jazz vocalist such as Ella Fitzgerald, Sarah Vaughan, Nat King Cole, or Frank Sinatra. Recordings for this purpose are easy to find on YouTube, Spotify, and other sources. After listening, follow up with specific questions for a brief class discussion. For example:

- Impression—Did you like it? Why or why not?
- Mood—Use one word to describe the mood (joyful, serious, exciting, sad, etc.).
- Energy—Rate the overall energy level on a scale of 1-5.
- Rhythm—Was it rhythmically inspiring? Did it make you want to tap your foot?
- Vocal—Was the vocal tone dark or light? Did the singer use vibrato?

Rhythmic Styles

There are a handful of different rhythmic styles frequently used in jazz music referred to as "grooves." Two of the most common are *swing feel* and *bossa nova*, differentiated primarily by contrasting eighth note subdivisions.

Bossa nova is a *straight* groove with each pair of eighth notes having an even subdivision:

Swing feel is a *swing* groove with each pair of eighth notes having a triplet subdivision:

These two grooves look exactly the same in notated music, but are felt differently in performance:

Rhythm Activity: Develop a better awareness of the difference between straight eighths and swing eighths with the following exercise. The goal is to maintain a steady tempo while alternating back and forth. First, tap (or step in tempo) quarter notes in a medium tempo. Then, speak the following in rhythm using a straight eighth feel:

Now tap (or step) quarter notes again and speak the following, this time using a swing eighth feel:

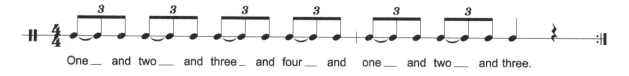

A fun next step is to make up short sentences, speaking straight and swing eighths in rhythm, switching back and forth between the two. Try this both ways:

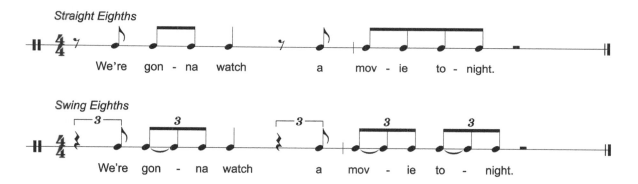

Performance Practice

Performance practice in vocal jazz usually involves a very conversational approach to lyric delivery. The general rule of thumb is "sing it like you say it." Here are just a few considerations.

- **Word Stress**—In everyday conversational speaking, strong emotional energy (excitement, frustration, etc.) usually goes hand in hand with pronounced word stress. The greater the emotional energy, the greater the word stress. This concept can be utilized by a vocal ensemble or soloist as a means to bump up the expression. In adhering to the "sing it like you say it" guideline: any word or syllable that might receive extra stress in conversation can also be stressed when singing.

FOREWORD *(continued)*

- **Vowels and Consonants**—The standards of excellence for choral music apply also to the vocal jazz aesthetic (excellent intonation, blend, tone color, clear diction, and so on). Still, there are a number of ways in which jazz must part ways with traditional choral conventions to be stylistically appropriate:

  1. Avoid exaggerated consonants such as heavy "K" or "P" plosives. Also, avoid the British hard "T" occurring in the middle or end of words such as "Water" and "Not."

  2. Allow vocal tone color to reflect the changing moods of the music. For example, highly energized rhythmic music may call for a brighter tone, while more gentle, intimate passages may call for rounder, warmer tones. Some phrases may call for a slightly breathy sound.

  3. Use vernacular speech as a guide to the pronunciation of most vowel sounds, avoiding vowel shapes that are highly modified from their original spoken counterpart. Short vowels, for example, "Fit," "Fed," "Fun," should stay generally true to normal conversation.

  4. Pronounce diphthongs just as they are in normal speaking when the notes are moving at a conversational pace. When diphthongs occur on long notes, observe the usual singing tradition of sustaining the first vowel sound as long as possible before moving to the secondary vowel.

- **Vibrato**—Vibrato is typically mitigated in vocal jazz, often to the point of being completely omitted. This practice may have developed as a strategy for achieving harmonic clarity within the dense chords and dissonances of jazz. For authentic group performance, avoiding vibrato is recommended. For soloists, use vibrato as a stylistic tool, especially at the end of long tones within ballads.

Scat Singing

Be sure to download the "Beginner's Guide to Scat Singing" (included with the Singer PDFs) for a step-by-step scat singing activity.

I hope that this short introduction will help you get the most out of your *Jazz Junior* experience and fall in love with the genre at the same time. Wishing you the very best on your musical journey!

Michele Weir

1. Bye Bye Blackbird

Arranged by
JAY ALTHOUSE

Words by **MORT DIXON**
Music by **RAY HENDERSON**

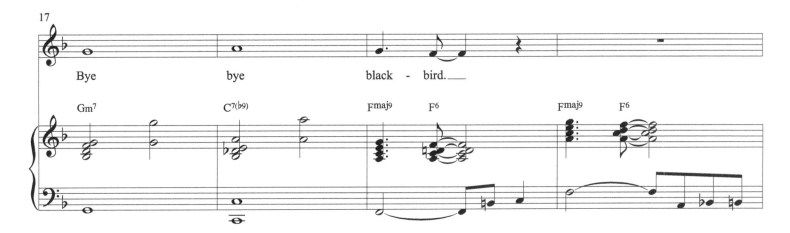

Make my bed and light the light;___ I'll ar-rive___ late to-night.___

Black - bird___ bye bye.

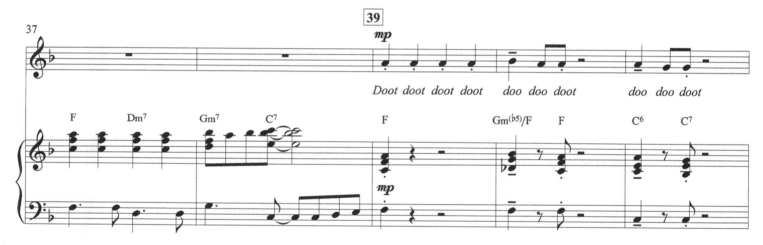

Doot doot doot doot doo doo doot doo doo doot

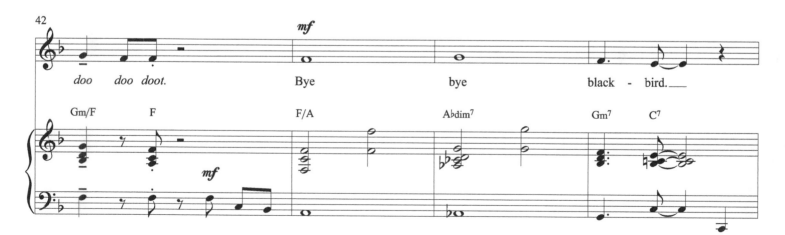

doo doo doot. Bye bye black - bird.___

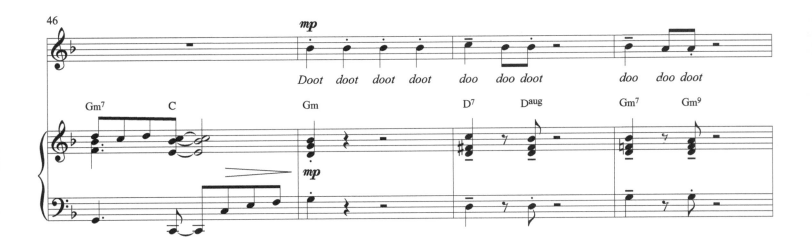

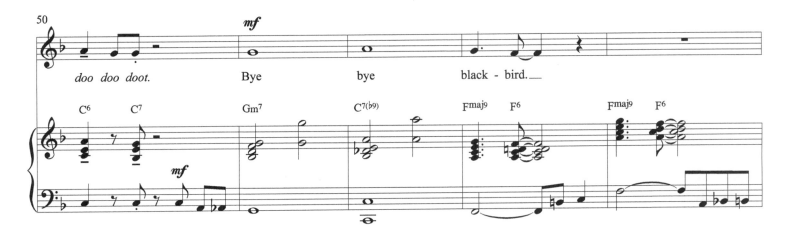

Make my bed and light the light;___ I'll ar-rive___ late to-night.___

Black - bird,_____ black - bird,_____

black - bird, bye bye, bye bye,

bye bye._____

2. Duke's Place

Arranged by
RUSSELL ROBINSON

Lyrics by **RUTH ROBERTS, BILL KATZ,**
and **ROBERT THIELE**
Music by **DUKE ELLINGTON**

Shoo ba doo ba doo bop.   Doot dot - n doo bop.

Sax - es   do their tricks at Duke's Place.

Fel - las   swing their chicks at Duke's Place.

Come on,   get your kicks in Duke's Place.

If you've nev - er been to Duke's Place,

take your toot-sies in - to Duke's Place.

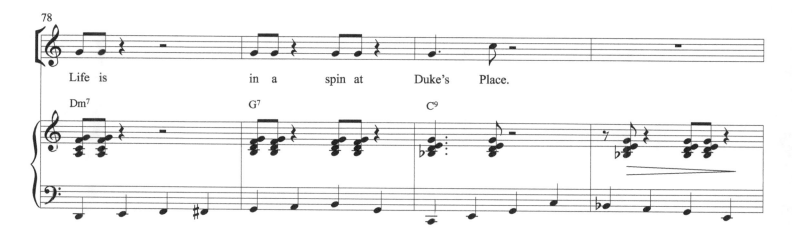

Life is in a spin at Duke's Place.

Life is in a spin at Duke's Place.

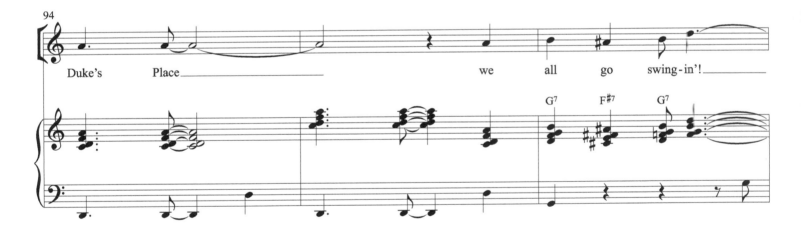

3. Fascinating Rhythm

Arranged by
MICHELE WEIR

Music and Lyrics by
GEORGE GERSHWIN *and* **IRA GERSHWIN**

49865

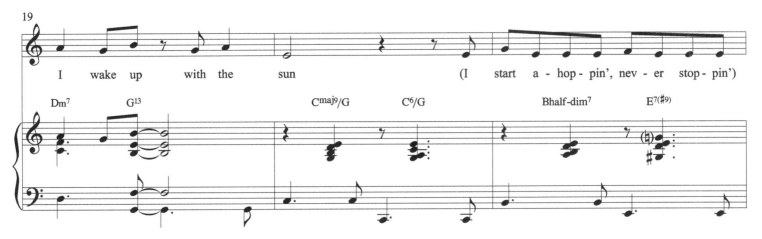

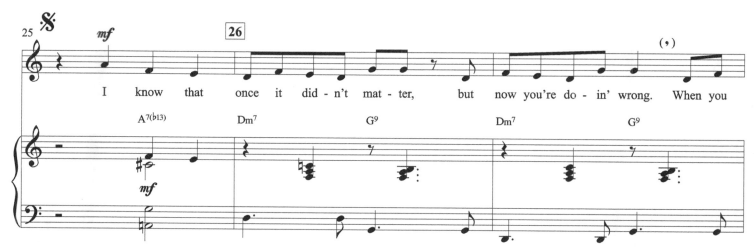

Oh, how I long to be____ the one____ I used to be.____

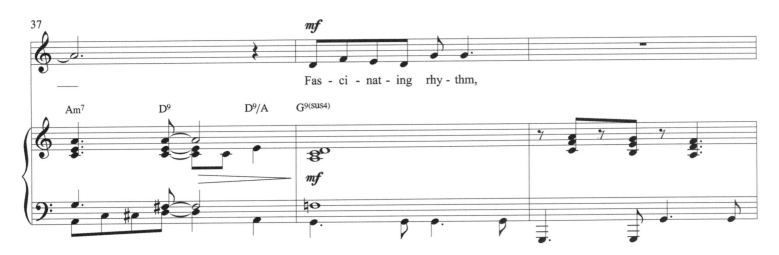

Fas - ci - nat - ing rhy - thm,

fas - ci - nat - ing rhy - thm, fas - ci - nat - ing rhy - thm,

2nd time to CODA
(p. 22, m. 61)

stop pick - in' on me!

Fas - ci - nat - ing rhy - thm you've got me on the go. Fas - ci -

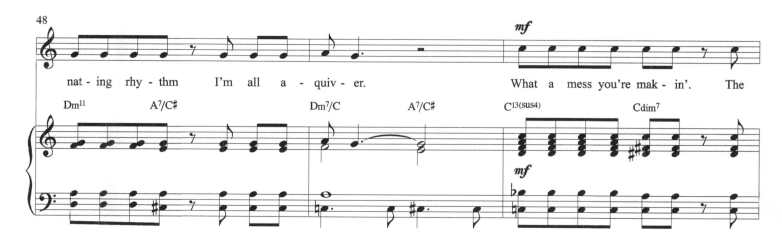

nat - ing rhy - thm I'm all a - quiv - er. What a mess you're mak - in'. The

neigh - bors want to know why I'm al - ways shak - in', just like a fliv - ver. ___

D.S. al CODA
(p. 19, m. 25)

Stop pick - in' on me!

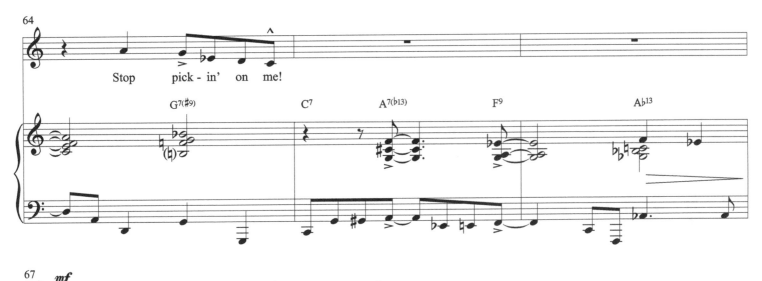

Stop pick - in' on me!

Got a lit - tle rhy - thm.   Stop pick - in' on me!

4. It Don't Mean a Thing
(If It Ain't Got That Swing)

Arranged by
MICHELE WEIR

Words by **IRVING MILLS**
Music by **DUKE ELLINGTON**

24

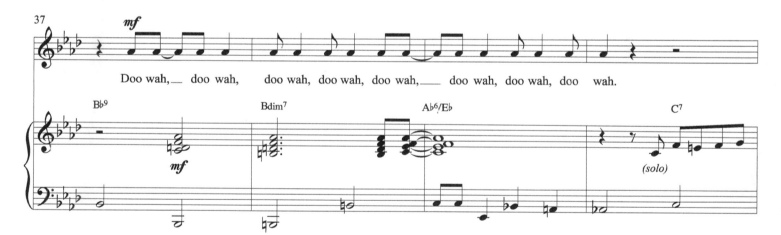

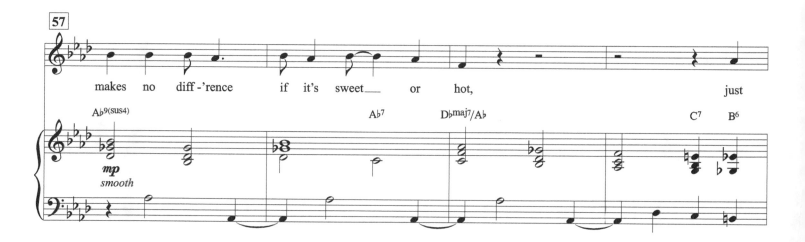

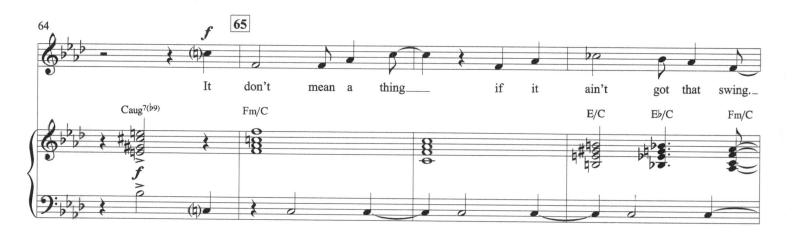

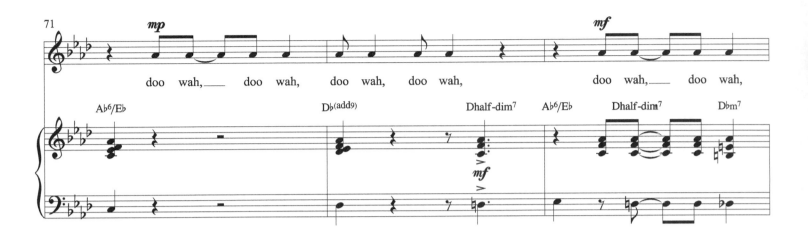

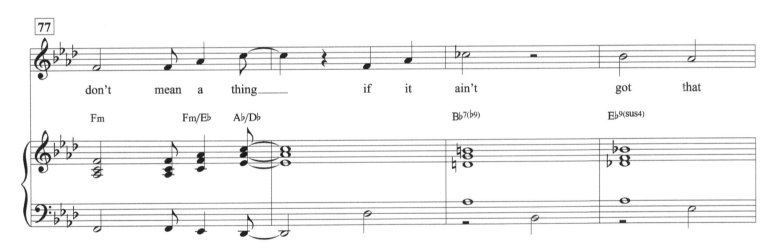

Singer Page 15

5. Jeepers Creepers

Arranged by
JAY ALTHOUSE

Words by **JOHNNY MERCER**
Music by **HARRY WARREN**

Lyrics:
I don't care what the weath-er-man says, when the weath-er-man says it's rain-ing. You'll nev-er hear me com-

49865

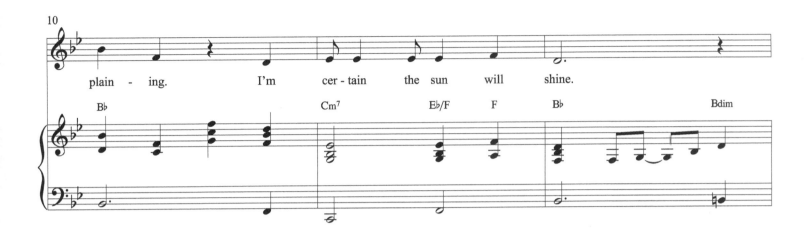

plain - ing. I'm cer - tain the sun will shine.

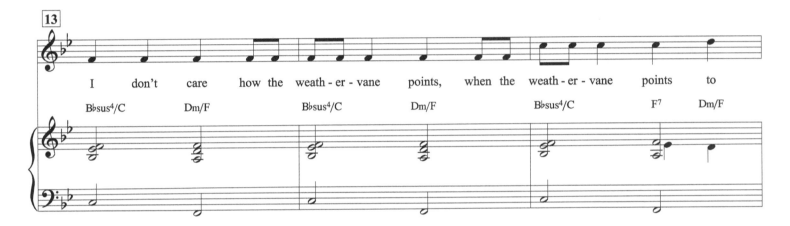

I don't care how the weath - er - vane points, when the weath - er - vane points to

gloom - y. It's got - ta be sun - ny to me, when your

eyes look in - to mine.

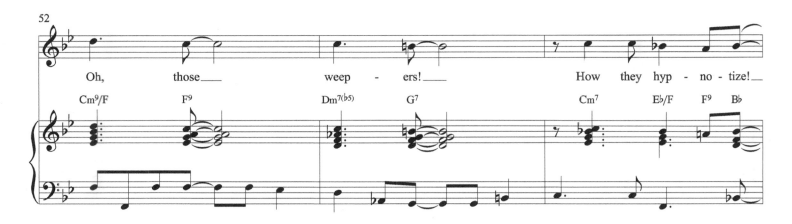

Bah doo bah doo dot, bah doo bah doo dot, bah doo bah doot dot

bah bah doo wow.___ Bah bah doo wah___ bah bah dah bah doo way.___

Where'd ya get those eyes? Gol - ly gee!___

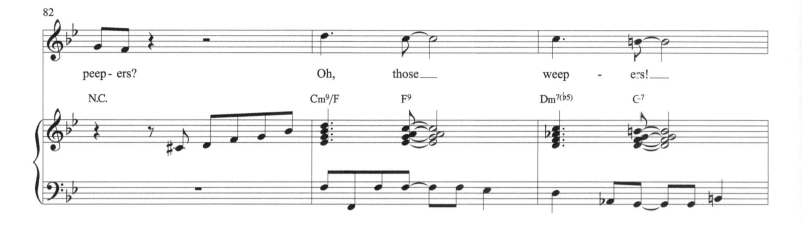

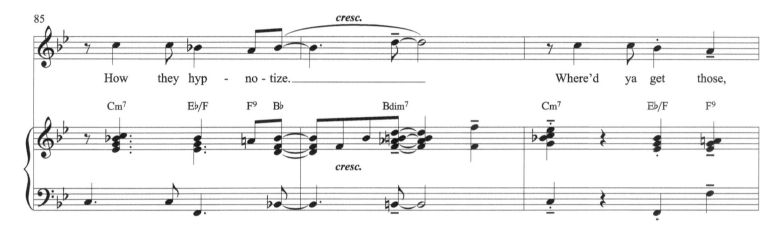

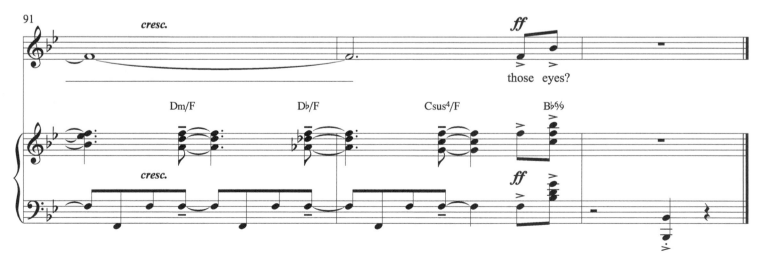

Singer Page 18

6. Let's Call the Whole Thing Off

Arranged by
RUSSELL ROBINSON

Music and Lyrics by
GEORGE GERSHWIN *and* **IRA GERSHWIN**

Ee - ther. Eye - ther. Nee - ther. Ny - ther. Let's call the whole thing

F / F7/Eb / Bb/D / Bbm/Db / F/C / Dm7

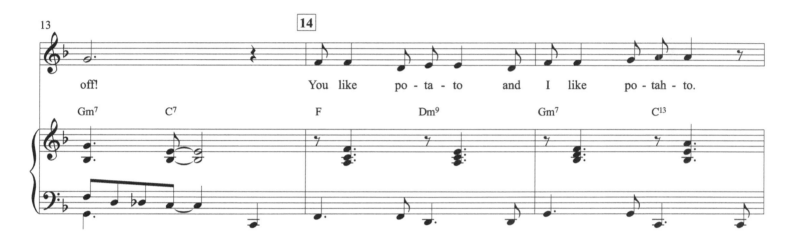

14

off! You like po - ta - to and I like po - tah - to.

Gm7 / C7 / F / Dm9 / Gm7 / C13

You like to - ma - to and I like to - mah - to. Po - ta - to. Po - tah - to. To -

F / Dm9 / Gm7 / C13 / F / F7/Eb

ma - to. To - mah - to. Let's call the whole thing off! But

Bb/D / Bbm/Db / F/C / Bb6/C / F

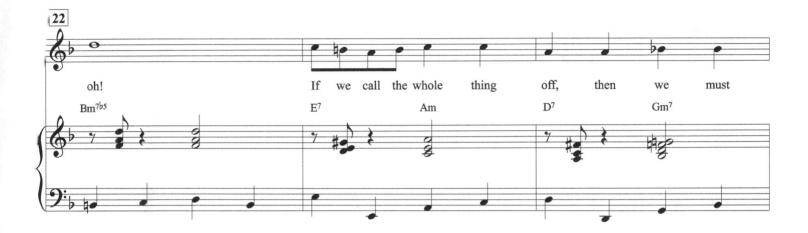

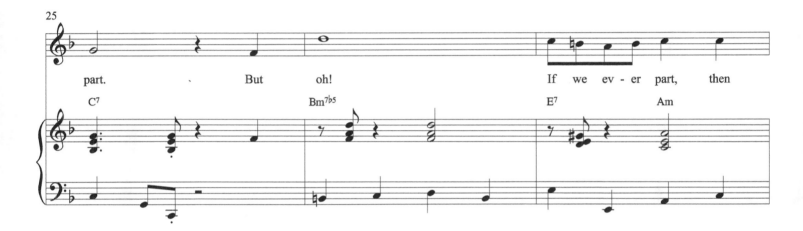

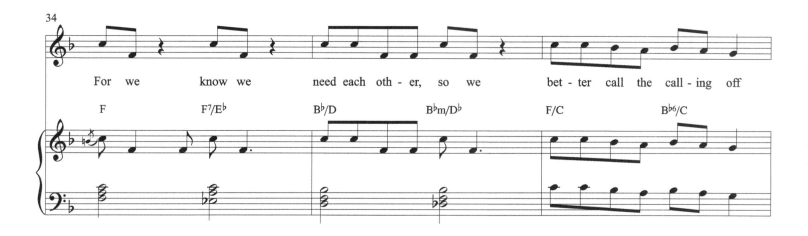

For we know we need each oth - er, so we bet - ter call the call - ing off

off. Let's call the whole thing off!

You say laugh - ter and I say lawf - ter.

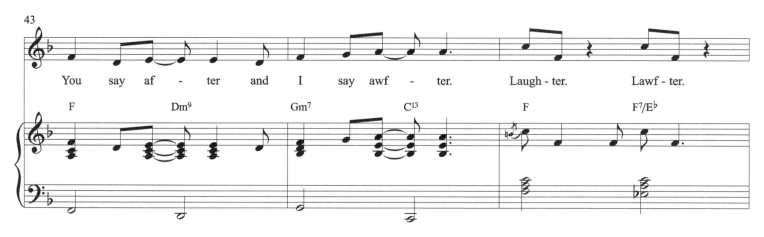

You say af - ter and I say awf - ter. Laugh - ter. Lawf - ter.

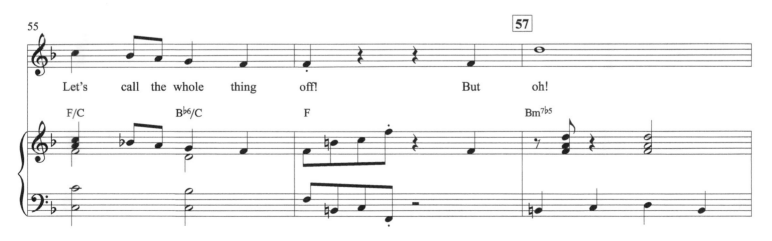

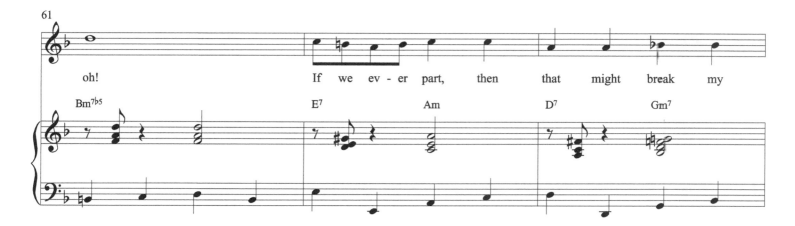

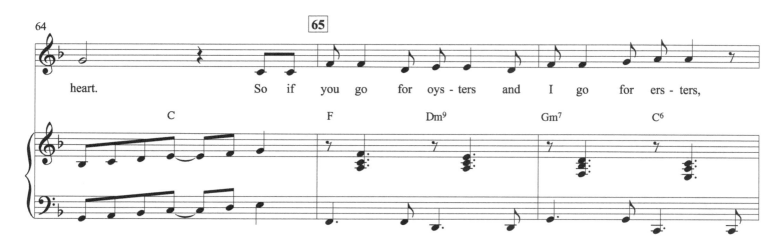

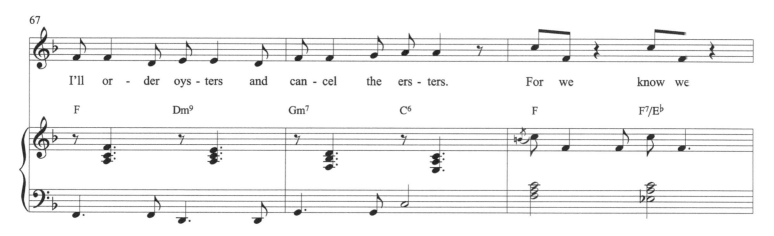

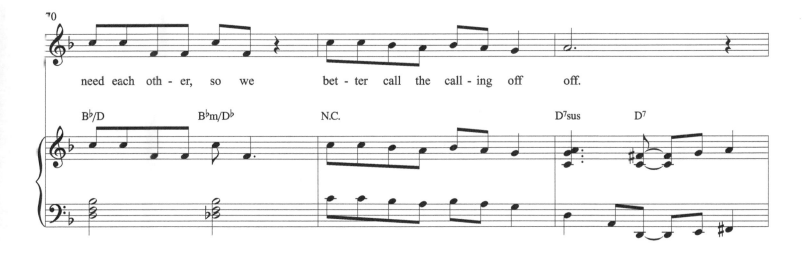

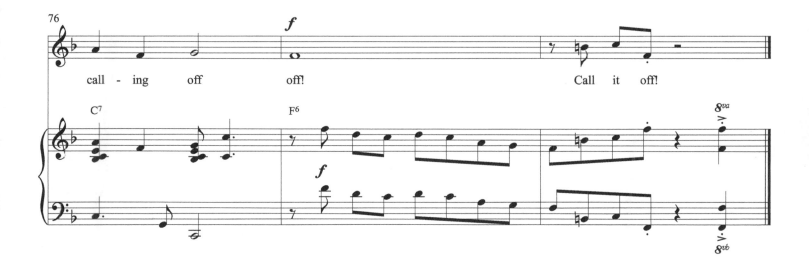

Singer Page 21

7. Misty

Arranged by
LISA DeSPAIN

Words by **JOHNNY BURKE**
Music by **ERROLL GARNER**

but it's just what I want you to do. Don't you no-tice how

hope-less-ly I'm lost? That's why I'm fol-low-ing

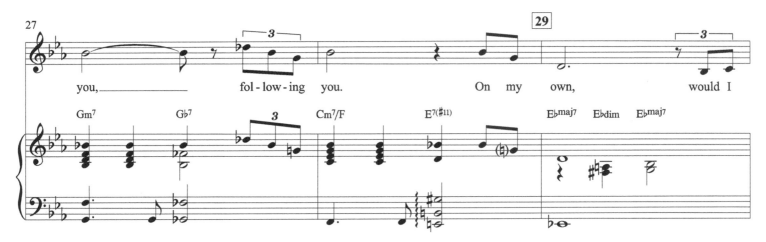

you,_____ fol-low-ing you. On my own, would I

wan-der_____ through this won-der-land a-lone? Nev-er know-ing my

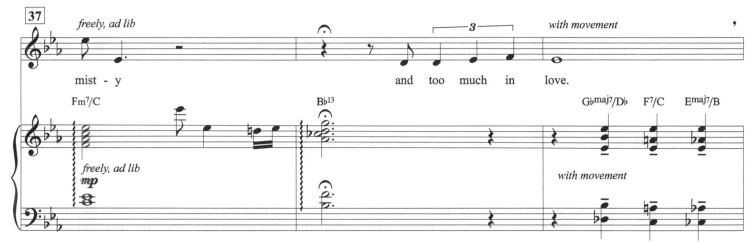

8. Orange Colored Sky

Arranged by
KIRBY SHAW

Words and Music by
MILTON DELUGG *and* **WILLIE STEIN**

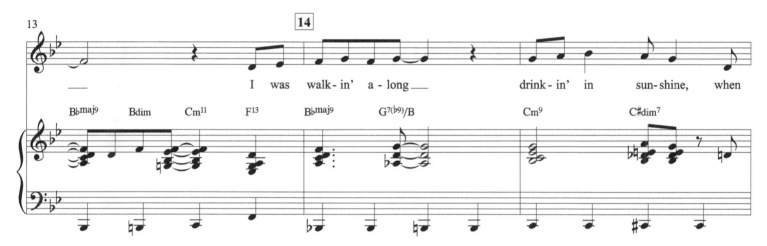

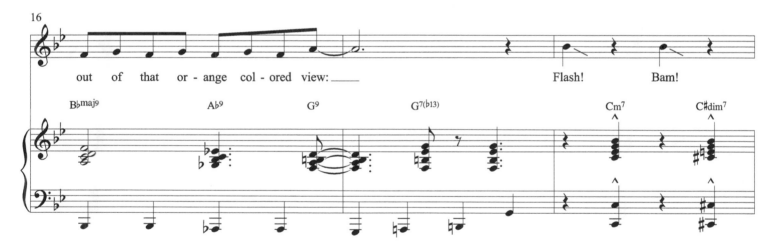

22 **𝄋**

One look and I yelled, "Tim - ber! Watch out for fly - ing glass!"

Eb6   Edim7   Am7(b5)   D7   Gm7

25

'Cause the ceil - ing fell in and the bot - tom fell out. I went

Gm   Gm/Gb

27

in - to a spin and I start - ed to shout, "I've been hit! This is it! This is

Gm/F   Em7(b5)   A7   F9   Cm9

cresc.

29   **30**

it!" Pow! __ I was walk - in' a - long __ mind - in' my bus -'ness, when

Cm7   F7   Bbmaj9   G7(b9)/B   Cm9   C#dim7

f   *mf*

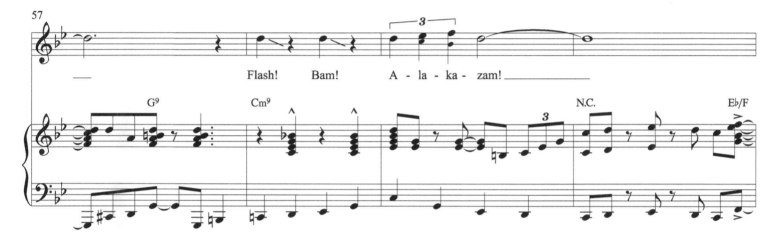

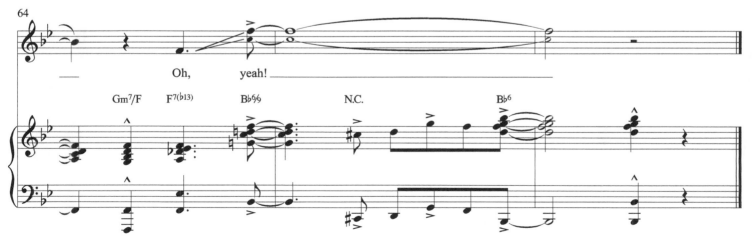

Singer Page 26

9. Over the Rainbow

Arranged by
KIRBY SHAW

Lyrics by **E. Y. HARBURG**
Music by **HAROLD ARLEN**

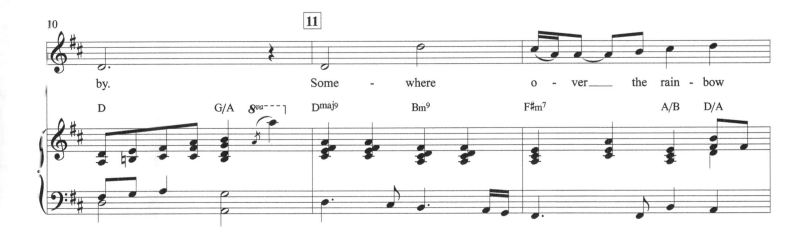

by. Some - where o - ver___ the rain - bow

skies are___ blue,___ and the

dreams that you dare to dream real - ly do come___ true. Some -

day I'll wish up - on a star___ and wake up where the clouds are far be - hind me.___

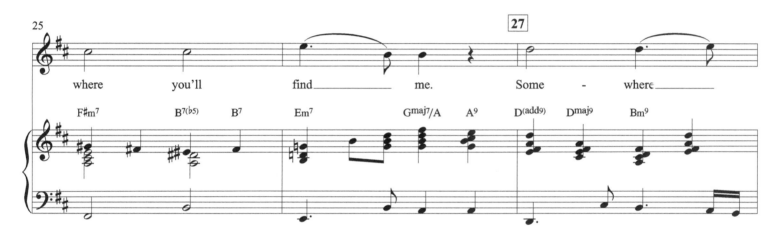

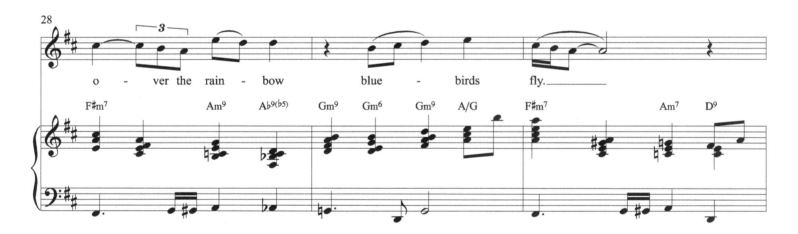

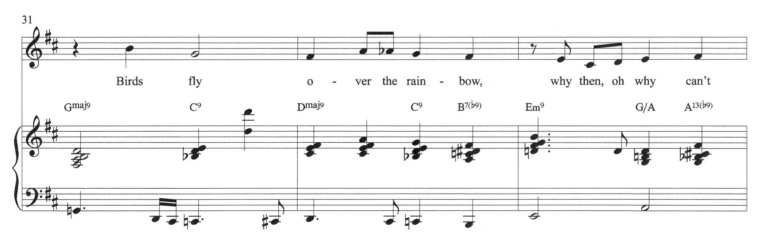

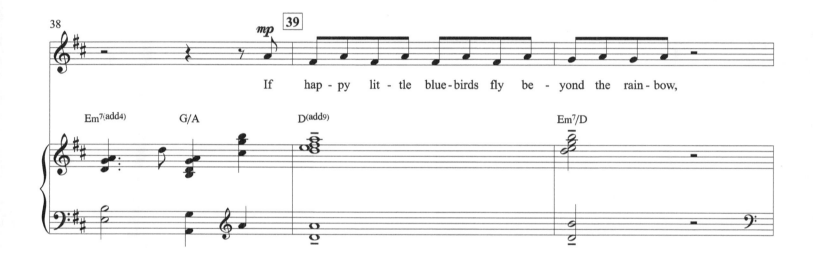

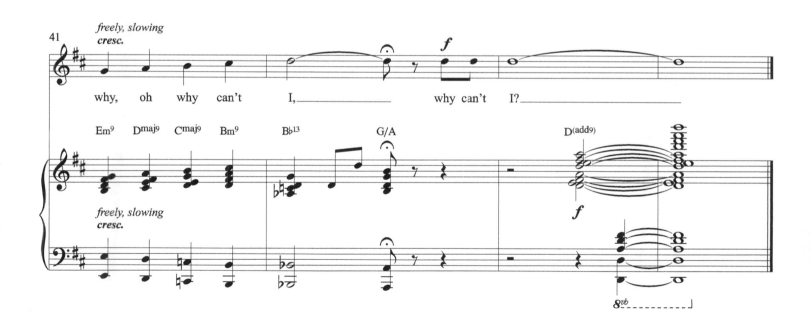

10. Straighten Up and Fly Right

Arranged by
LISA DeSPAIN

Words and Music by
NAT KING COLE *and* **IRVING MILLS**

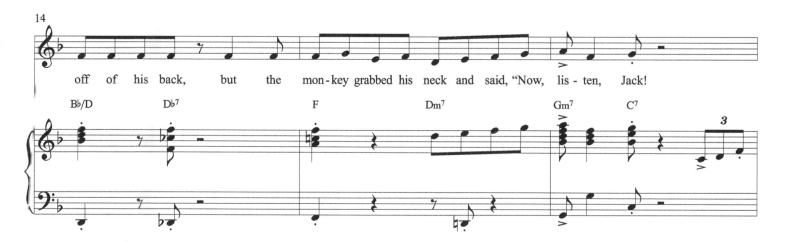

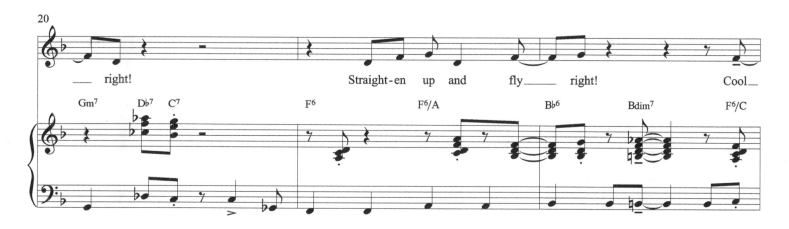

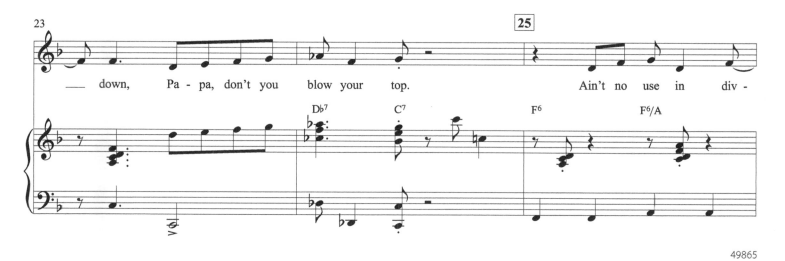

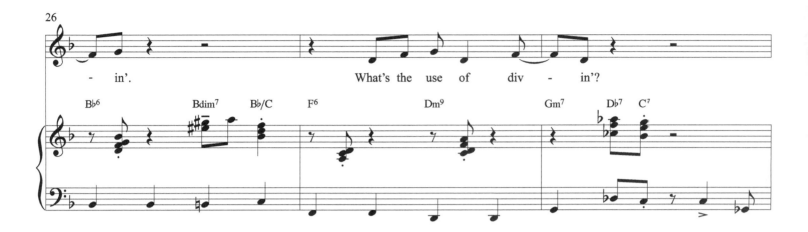

- in'. What's the use of div - in'?

Straight-en up and fly___ right! Cool___ down, Pa - pa, don't you

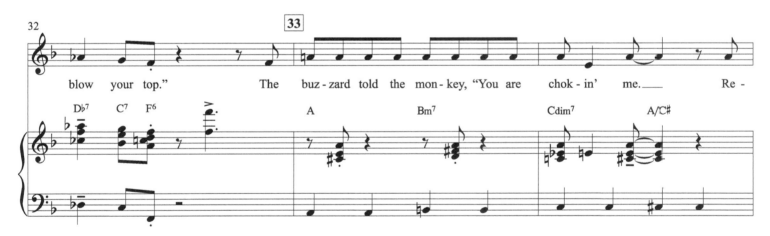

blow your top." The buz - zard told the mon - key, "You are chok - in' me.___ Re -

lease your hold___ and I will set you free."___ The mon - key looked the buz - zard right

dead in the eye,___ said, "Your sto - ry's so touch - in', but it sounds like a lie.

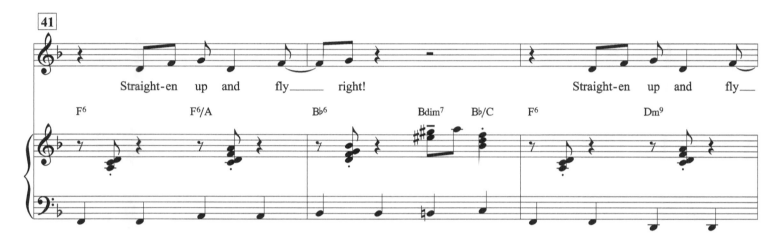

Straight-en up and fly___ right! Straight-en up and fly___

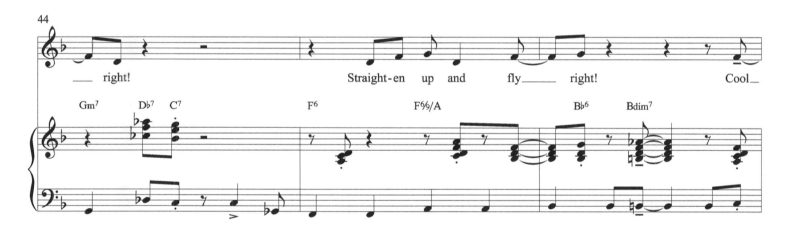

___ right! Straight-en up and fly___ right! Cool___

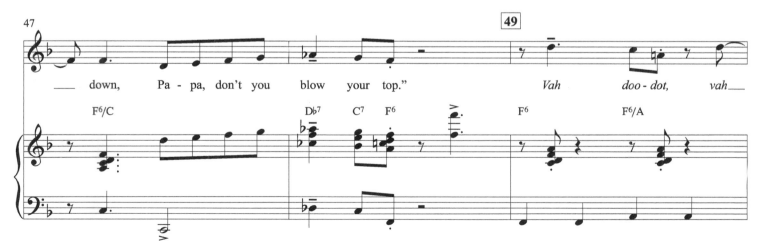

___ down, Pa - pa, don't you blow your top." Vah doo - dot, vah___

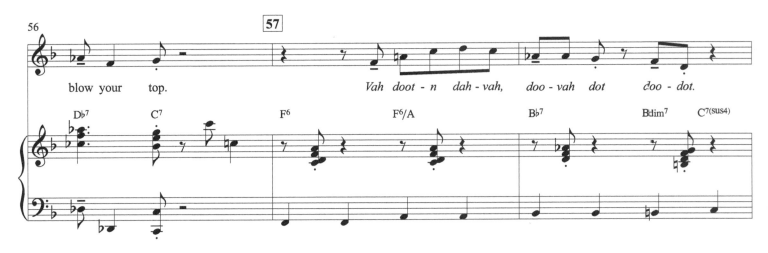

doo - vah, doo - vah, doo - dot. Cool___ down, Pa - pa, don't you blow your top. The

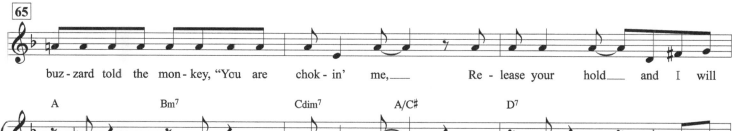

buz - zard told the mon - key, "You are chok - in' me,___ Re - lease your hold___ and I will

set you free."___ The mon - key looked the buz - zard right dead in the eye,___ said, "Your

sto - ry's so touch - in', but it sounds like a lie. Straight-en up and fly___

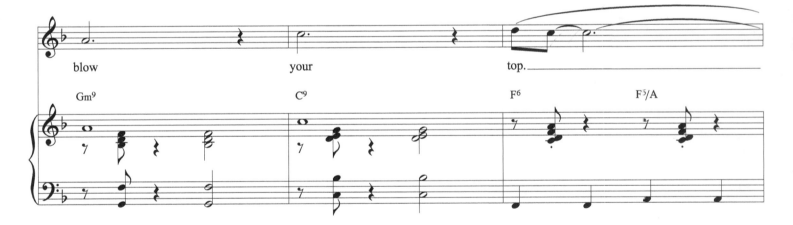

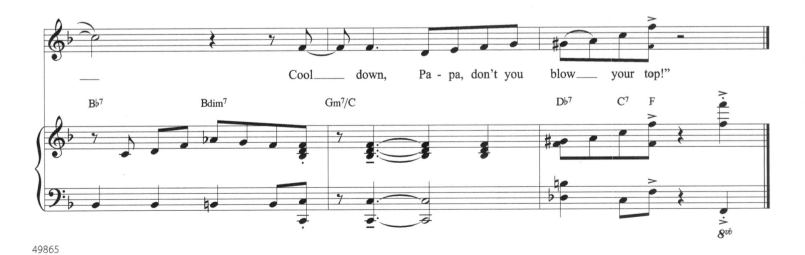